# STAINED GLASS

## Inspirations and Designs

# STAINED GLASS

## Inspirations and Designs

### Terrance Plowright

Front cover: *Gathering of the Most Sacred*, a 213 cm (7') diameter leadlight window made
from American Cathedral glass (see page 12)
Frontispiece: Detail of *Sacred Connection*, a large leadlight window of mostly German and
French Antique glass (see page 29)

*Reprinted in paperback 1994*
*First published in 1993 by Kangaroo Press Pty Ltd*
*3 Whitehall Road Kenthurst NSW 2156 Australia*
*P.O. Box 6125 Dural Delivery Centre NSW 2158*
*Typeset by G.T. Setters Pty Limited*
*Printed in Singapore through Global Com Pte Ltd*

ISBN 0 86417 660 0

# Contents

Foreword        7

Introduction        9

Photo gallery        11

Working with stained glass        41

    Environments for stained glass        41

    Handling glass and lead        42

    Reinforcing—a new way        43

    Enlarging a design        44

Designs        45

    Design guidelines        46

Finale        101

Index        104

Detail from *Energy* (page 21), a work created from slab glass *(dalle de virre)* using a hammer and chisel

# Foreword

Stained glass has been with us for many centuries. It has been used in cathedrals and other religious buildings worldwide, both to illustrate biblical stories for those who could not read and to inspire religious experience in its viewers. In concert with grand architecture and huge vaulted ceilings, stained glass, filling vast open spaces with colours lit by the sun, has traditionally held an important place in our spiritual and artistic life.

Now there is a new direction, a new opening—and a tremendously revitalised art and industry is blossoming, revealing many new and wonderful possibilities. Stained glass, a symphony of colour and light inspiring and uplifting with glory and grandeur, softening and mood-setting, whatever the space or use, constantly changing and playing with the light of day, will be with us for many more centuries. Many of the works created today may still be here a thousand years from now, just as many of the great windows of colour and light from yesteryear adorn our older buildings today.

My hope is that this book will be an inspiration and will enrich your appreciation of the art, or will be an encouragement to become involved, to design and create stained glass. I would also hope that it will be yet another hint to think passionately about what it is you do with your life, as I believe we all have untapped potential to bring into being the new architecture, new physics, new philosophy, music, sculpture, film and art, and at the same time be aware that the art or stained glass of now will become tomorrow's history and our benchmark, measuring from whence we have come and giving those in the future an insight into who we were and the works, quality and measure of our day.

Detail from *Purity of Spirit* (page 102) showing the wonderful prismatic effects caused by light striking the bevelled edges

# Introduction

This book first and foremost is about contemporary stained glass. I hope it will inspire you as well as provide you with an opportunity to develop another skill designing your own stained glass.

I have divided the book into two sections, the first being photographs of a cross-section of my own stained glass innovations, giving you an overview of what one artist has so far done in the contemporary field. I also talk about some pitfalls and associated design problems, as well as pointing out practical ways of overcoming these problems. The second section contains simple and not-so-simple designs for your own use.

My hope is that this book will say something to everyone interested in the arts, to the very beginner stained glass student as well as to those who are a little more advanced in stained glass design. And just briefly I would like to touch on an area of thought that has interested me throughout much of my adult life, and that is human potential—the ability to open up new possibilities, and if you feel for something, to get in and have a go.

I walked into my first stained glass studio at the age of 31, delivered by an American friend who was himself becoming internationally renowned as an artist in glass. My first response to the studio was quiet interest, but I grew more excited as we strolled around, viewing the photographs on the walls—some were of works designed and built by the studio, others contemporary works designed by famous German and American stained glass artists.

I had just arrived back from America and was feeling at a loose end, so I enrolled in a stained glass night class. I thought this would occupy a few hours while I explored the possibility of a new direction in my life. My first night in the class was awful! I couldn't cut the glass; even the easy-to-cut practice glass broke in all the wrong places. I recall seeing everyone else in the class, working away, cutting with great competence, while I was feeling very vulnerable and creating the most dreadful mess.

My second evening was almost as bad but I did manage to score (a glass-working term meaning 'cut') a few pieces of glass successfully. Another problem that surfaced in the second evening was waiting for my tutor to come to my aid. In the end, after three evenings of much waiting, I left the class and bought a book.

At the same time I was contacted by another friend. He had heard that I was involved in a stained glass course, and offered to buy my materials if I would design and build a stained glass window for his new home. This I did with great passion, working away day and night. Then came a call from Robert Middlestead, a Canadian friend, offering a place in his studio as his lackey. I jumped at the chance and in three weeks I was on a plane winging my way into a new adventure, an adventure with stained glass (and more), and since then I have not looked back. Twelve months down the track I opened my own studio. Five years further on and many commissions completed, some prestigious, I began to explore the world of sculpture and painting.

As a youth I had no idea all this was inside me—I had no idea that an ability in sculpture, painting and stained glass lay hidden, waiting to reveal itself, and I have no idea what is going to open up next. I am loving my work—every new commission is an exciting opportunity to create, whether it be sculpture, stained glass or this book.

So, if you wish to do something for your home, give stained glass a try ... If you follow a few basic rules you cannot go wrong—and who knows what it might lead to or uncover in you. You may find a new and exciting passion which will direct you to many other opportunities or adventures in many other areas of life, not just as recreation but as new areas of creativity. It may even lead to a new profession and a greater sense of satisfaction and wholeness.

Over the years I have taught many students and I would have to say that very few have felt comfortable on the first night. Most are a little concerned about the glass. It *is* sharp! Yet I would also say that I have never witnessed a bad cut from glass and I have not had one student who after some practice and the exercise of a little patience could not cut the glass with some competence—and some of my students have been as old as nine and as young as seventy.

Over the path of my own life I have been involved with many people—friends, students, family and professional acquaintances—and it has never ceased to amaze me how we do seem to get so stuck. We create fortresses in our minds, in our hearts and literally on the earth where we live, yet there is, as long as we are in reasonable health, a huge number of opportunities enabling us to explore the world in which we live as well as the creativity that lives in us. I do hope this book is of some value to you, maybe even an inspiration to those who take the time to look through these pages. In any case I am delighted to have been asked to put something like this together as it has opened up another opportunity for me to explore something new. I would be delighted if it provides for you an opportunity to examine a new possibility, bringing light, colour and a new skill into your life with the limitless world of stained glass.

Opening up new directions . . .

*Listening* by Terrance Plowright

Bronze, 1 m high

Einstein once said that it is impossible to solve a problem at the level from which it was created. It was this statement, to some extent, that inspired my work with these particular sculptural forms.

The three figures represent the receptive—the ability to hear, the quality of emptiness and the dissolving of ignorance. Within this quality of living, without a need to be right, or a need to belong to any one point of view, I believe space is created, and in that space one has the opportunity to operate with some intelligence, and if quiet, to be filled with immensity.

# Photo gallery

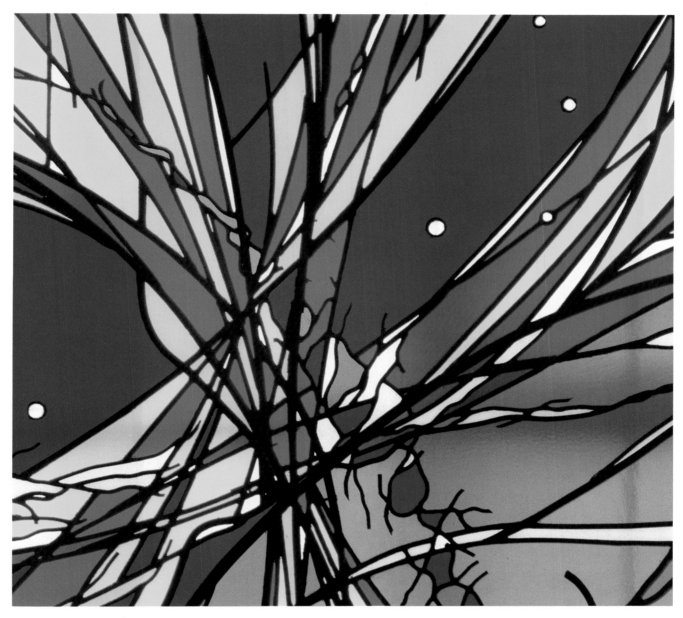

Detail of *Gathering of the Most Sacred*. Note the false leading. This can add a great deal to a design, especially if the work is contemporary.

## Gathering of the Most Sacred

*Size:* 213 cm (7') diameter
*Glass:* American Cathedral
*Technique:* Leadlight

Note the clear glass globules (stars). They have been copper foiled and soldered into cavities which were ground through the glass with an ordinary studio glass grinder. Note the lovely splay of colour across the floor thrown out by natural light passing through the stained glass.

This window was specially designed and built for the World Council of Churches exhibition in Australia.

No definable reinforcing line spoils the flow of line and colour in this work. The main strength is behind the window where a web of steel bar has been bent to shape along the lead line. The steel bar was hot dipped in tin so it could be soldered to the lead came. The process, which is quite time consuming but highly rewarding artistically, is discussed in detail on page 42.

## White Gums

*Size:* 229 × 122 cm (7'6'' × 4')
*Glass:* German Antique, French Antique and American Kokomo
*Technique:* Copper foil

Opposite above:

## Clydesdales

*Size:* 244 × 183 cm (8' × 6')
*Glass:* French Antique, German Antique and American Bullseye (1400 pieces)
*Technique:* Leadlight, some painted areas

Opposite below:

## Untitled

*Size:* 244 × 168 cm (8' × 5'6'')
*Glass:* French Antique and German Antique
*Technique:* Leadlight

## Garrison Memorial

The Rocks, Sydney
*Size:* 335 × 183 cm (11' × 6')
*Glass:* German Antique and American Cathedral
*Technique:* Leadlight

Stained glass is not only about designing and building windows. It's also about communication and I can assure you that there will be times when your very best skills in this area will be called into play. In regard to the *Garrison Memorial*, I first had to deal with the group which had put forward the finance, working on themes and a design style that was acceptable. Then we had to work through the committee of architects at the Sydney Cove Redevelopment Authority, after which we went back to the original architects through whom the commission came. When these three bodies were happy we then had to confer with the church minister and finally with the church committee. So you see, commission work is not always straightforward.

From my time as a small boy I have been deeply saddened by war, by the deep river of human blood which runs so violently through our history. Soldiers have died in their millions, women and children have suffered terribly, dying themselves or dying in spirit from the loss of husbands, fathers, brothers, friends.

In my work I wanted to convey my own sadness, through the figure, which is neither male nor female. It transmits a deep sadness for those lost but also represents the dead, ghostly, contemplatively hovering over the grave. The weapon of war — the rifle — is shown at rest. To the left and right is the curtain, nurturing enveloping sadness, softening the loss death has delivered and yet itself stained with blood. And above is the sun, a symbol of illumination and the pouring out of new life.

## Cronulla

*Size:* 244 × 91 cm (8' × 3')
*Glass:* American Cathedral
*Technique:* Leadlight

*Sun Sail*
*Size:* 305 × 91 cm (10' × 3')
*Glass:* American Cathedral
*Technique:* Leadlight

Opposite:

*Clasping Hands*
*Size:* 122 × 91 cm (4' × 3')
*Glass:* French Antique
*Technique:* Leadlight

Note: Lead came is epoxied to
the glass

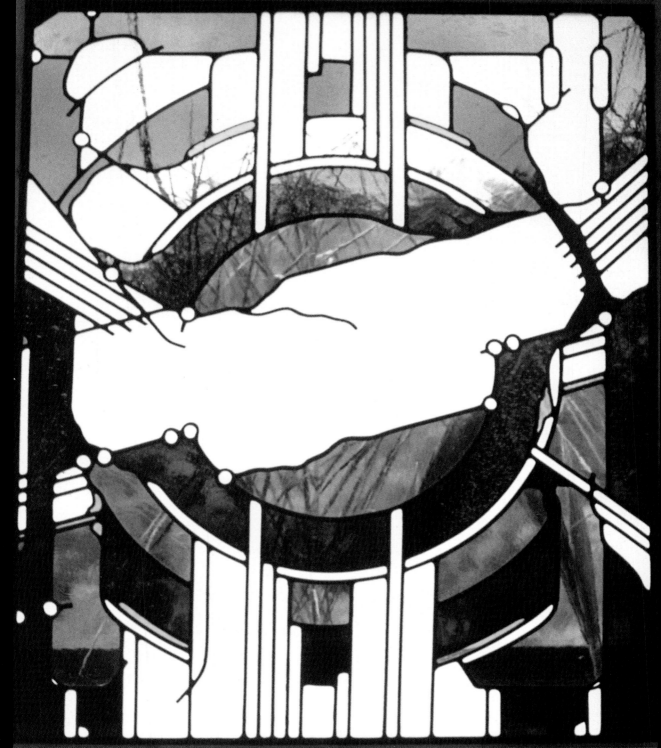

## Kookaburras

*Size:* 107 cm (3'6'') diameter
*Glass:* American Cathedral
*Technique:* Leadlight

Opposite:

## Energy

*Size:* 229 × 122 cm (7'6'' × 4'')
*Glass:* French Slab and American Slab
*Technique: Dalle de virre*

This particular work was created using a hammer and chisel.
I personally find this technique most exciting. The glass comes
in slabs 30 cm long, 20 cm wide, 2.5 cm thick (12'' long,
8'' wide, 1'' thick) which are then cut or chiselled to size.
In this panel I have also cut some of the small thin pieces
with a diamond saw. Traditionally the slabs were placed
together in a cement solution but now there are new epoxy
resins available which have the same coefficient expansion rate
as the glass slabs. This prevents cracking, which was one of
the most common problems experienced with the old
technique using common cement.

22

*Echo Point*
*Size:* 107 cm (3'6'') diameter
*Glass:* French Antique and German Antique
*Technique:* Leadlight

Opposite:

## Banksias

*Size:* 107 cm (3'6'') diameter
*Glass:* French Antique and German Antique
*Technique:* Leadlight

## Waratahs

*Size:* 107 cm (3'6'') diameter
*Glass:* German Antique
*Technique:* Leadlight

## Uriah Heep

*Size:* 183 × 152 cm (6' × 5')
*Glass:* In this particular work we used a large number of different types of glass including German Antique, French Antique, Kokomo, Bullseye, Spectrum and some old Merry Go Round which I had had lying around for some years—nearly 1000 pieces of glass.
*Technique:* Leadlight

Note the lack of visual reinforcing—the whole stained glass window is totally unencumbered. Normally with a work of this size you would break the window up into six sections so the design would have reinforcing lines running throughout. We have also accomplished various effects with some elementary painting, mainly simple trace and mat techniques with a little silver stain around the hair. All the writing is simple trace work and if you look closely enough you can see that every book has a title. Obviously this window took an enormous number of hours, from the very beginning of the design stage to the complex and time consuming reinforcing, but the result was most satisfying. Just to give you some idea of the time involved, specially in the use of this new system of reinforcing—for this one window it took some 30 hours to bend the bar and solder it to the lead; if I remember rightly the whole window from start to finished grossed about 240 hours.

Opposite:
Detail from *Uriah Heep*

24

## Artful Dodger

*Size:* 183 × 152 cm (6' × 5')
*Glass:* As in *Uriah Heep*, a combination of Antique and Cathedral glass.
*Technique:* Leadlight

This window involved some elementary painting—not as much as the *Uriah Heep* work—but it has over 1400 pieces of glass. A similar time was amassed for this window: around 240 hours.

26

## Untitled

*Size:* 244 × 91 cm (8' × 3')
*Glass:* German Antique
*Technique:* Leadlight

Note the use of a very lightly tinted Antique glass which enables the outside, the beautiful garden with its lovely greens and blossom colours, to be brought inside. This is a technique I have used often, with the result here being quite delightful.

## African Stag

*Size:* 213 × 79 cm (7' × 2'7'')
*Glass:* American Cathedral
*Technique:* Leadlight

## Bursting Through

*Size:* 549 cm high, 91 cm wide at the base and 213 cm across the horizontal (18' high, 3' at base, 7' across the horizontal)
*Glass:* French Antique and German Antique
*Technique:* Leadlight

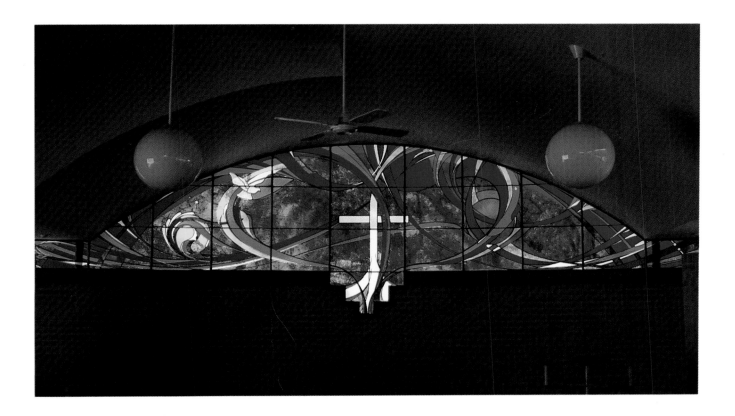

Opposite:

While I was working on *Bursting Through* I became extremely aware of the powerful form of the cross. It symbolises so many different concepts or ideas that in today's Christian world it has been dismissed by some as irrelevant. In fact I have worked on religious designs for some well known mainstream groups which have insisted on its non-appearance. The cross as a symbol predates the time of Christ; in early thinking it was used as a symbol to identify the meeting place between the superficial and the profound—the horizontal represented the Earth or the superficial and the vertical represented the depth, the inner, the profound. So today it is treated dismissively by some, or is seen as symbolic of suffering. Being aware of some of the symbolism and history of the cross, and feeling the power it had, and still does have, for literally millions of people, I wanted to break through and generate an experience in the observer of inspiration, of breaking out, of opening to the new and leaving behind our link with the past.

I offer this, my own experience, to open up some insight into the process of, not just the designing, but what leads to design, what is behind the work. I would be surprised if this process did not go on in the minds and hearts of most artists. I know it is certainly behind most of my work, whether it be sculpture, stained glass or painting, and surely it's this process that enriches our lives, leading to great and passionate outpourings of works down through the ages.

## Sacred Connection

*Size:* 15.25 m × 3.7 m (50' × 12')
*Glass:* Mostly German and French Antique, with a little American Cathedral to the sides
*Technique:* Leadlight

This window is quite large and even though I have broken the design up into many segments, these segments are at least 1 to 1.3 square metres (9 to 12 square feet) each, hence we also used the new reinforcing technique which was welded to the main steel frame. Again, looking at what's behind this work, my client was very keen on symbolism and the symbols commonly used in the Christian world. So I tried to tie together a lot of the symbols offered—images of the cross, the dove, the fish, the peoples of different countries, black, white, yellow, images of the earth, the sun, the Bible, the Eucharist, all in together, connected by sweeping lines of colour and form. There is a small forest outside this church which is discernible through the Antique glass and brings to worship a gentle reminder that our connection with the natural world, with the great beauty of nature, is absolutely paramount in our meditation and/or worship together today. Here again I have tried to work with the client's needs, yet I was allowed certain freedoms in the design which made this project most enjoyable.

## Pretty Straight

*Size:* 549 cm × 183 cm (18' × 6')
*Glass:* American Kokomo
*Technique:* Leadlight

Budget plays an important role in design and in the choice of glass. This window had a small budget for its size. (In fact most windows fall into this category.) You have to work within a budget. At times I find this quite difficult but it is absolutely imperative that you learn the skill of working to your budget or that will deliver great hardship throughout your career. As an older stained glass artist told me when I first opened my studio, ninety per cent of all the studios that open up close down within two years. 'Why?' I asked. 'Not being fast enough and not having the ability to stick to budgets.'

It's very sobering to look at a space, become excited and suddenly see the incredible things you could do, then to be told your budget is less than half of what you had hoped for. This brings your expectations crashing to earth and your marvellous ideas to a dead stop. In fact, now I do not even consider what can be done until I am fully aware of all the facts, and that definitely includes budget.

In the commercial world you can look at this compromise and restraint as a challenge. We will for some time yet have to face the fact that we live in Australia and Australians, especially those in the business of building buildings, are only grudgingly coerced into providing funds for art works. One only has to go to Europe or North America to see how deprived we are of public art (sculpture, stained glass, etc.). So, for the time being at least, small budgets are what you will have to work with for the most part. And, I might add, I am very grateful for the opportunities I've had to date—even when small budgets are all that's available, at least you have been given a job and an opportunity to flex your artistic muscle.

## Ibis

*Size:* 213 × 61 cm (7' × 2'), 2 panels
*Glass:* American Kokomo
*Technique:* Leadlight

In designing these windows I was inspired by a large abstract painting which hung on the wall to one side of them. I also worked the design to blend in with a huge wrought iron gate which is very visible when the front door is open, which I was led to believe is quite often. This is another example of working with what is there, the architecture, plus the inside and outside environment.

*Living Water*
*Size:* 244 × 183 cm (8' × 6')
*Glass:* French Antique and German Antique
*Technique:* Copper foil

This work uses nearly 1000 pieces of glass and is reinforced using the bent steel bar method. Note the many strands of false solder strips which are glued to the glass with epoxy.

Opposite:
Detail of *Living Water*

Opposite:

## Snooker table light shade

*Size:* 213 × 61 cm (7' × 2')
*Glass:* American Cathedral
*Technique:* Leadlight

This lamp shade was built into a timber frame which, I might add, cost an arm and a leg. The result was most rewarding and my client was very happy. However, my friend who was responsible for building the timber frame gave my client a firm quote and then proceeded to go three times over budget! I was very grateful that he carried through (being a professional I'm sure he did not make the same mistake twice), even though he did not speak to me ever again. (Only kidding!) This was one of those rare problems that arise from time to time— even though he is extremely skilled at fine timber work, it was impossible to foresee the number of difficult joints that would be needed, and there were sixty-three of them. This relates to stained glass work in as far as it relates to the ability to keep to budget—sometimes with the best intentions in the world you will run over because you have entered an area that is unfamiliar. Just be sure to complete the job and count it as a learning experience. You may be lucky to find a client who will go halfway on the cost overruns, but don't push it or you may gain a reputation which may haunt you for years to come.

I decided to include this particular shade as an example, because it is reasonably simple to design for flat surfaces rather than the traditionally rounded or moulded copperfoil shade; as long as the frame is strong and large enough you can create to your heart's content. The only thing you must look out for when designing this particular type of shade is the way the sides cast shadows over the snooker table. It would be wise to make a mockup in cardboard with a light inside to see where the sides will throw shadow. Don't be put off by this task—it's easy—and once this aspect is worked out and you have found someone skilled enough to make the frame, the rest is plain sailing.

Right:

## As Light Falls

*Size:* 213 × 61 cm (7' × 2')
*Glass:* American Cathedral
*Technique:* Leadlight

This window was designed to fill the function of a small partition, but could easily have been placed as a side light. Again it was to a small budget, so I chose an inexpensive glass and a simple but quiet and elegant flow of line.

## The Cave

*Size:* 100 cm (3'4'') diameter
*Glass:* French Antique and German Antique
*Technique:* Leadlight

Note the use of lightly tinted Antique glass to bring the outside in; the outside being almost forest, it would have been silly to have wasted it. This is a simple design for a simple budget.

## Bullocks Flat Ski Tube

*Size:* 396 × 183 cm (13' × 6')
*Glass:* American Cathedral, with some Antique
*Technique:* Leadlight

Within this autonomous work I have incorporated many symbols from the local environment: Bullocks Flat Terminal, the Ski Tube, Mt Perisher, the Swiss cross (which is also similar to the cross worn by ski rescue team members), the Southern Cross, ski slopes, among others. All of these symbols have been tied together with flowing lines and colour.

When facing a blank sheet of paper and a specific task, if your choice is to go abstract but not pure abstract, I suggest you lay out all the possible symbols pertaining to the project and get stuck in, working them together, playing around with them. See how they run together—eventually you will come to something that is pleasing—but always keep in the back of your mind the budget.

This window was designed and built before I knew about the new system of bending hot dipped steel and soldering to the lead came described on page 42. So I had a friend bend some steel rod to the shape of the flowing lines throughout the window, which were then screwed into the main frame and wired to each panel. Hence no unbroken line or intruding reinforcing rod is visible.

## Untitled

*Size:* 244 × 61 cm (8' × 2'), 2 panels
*Glass:* German Antique and French Antique
*Technique:* Leadlight

38

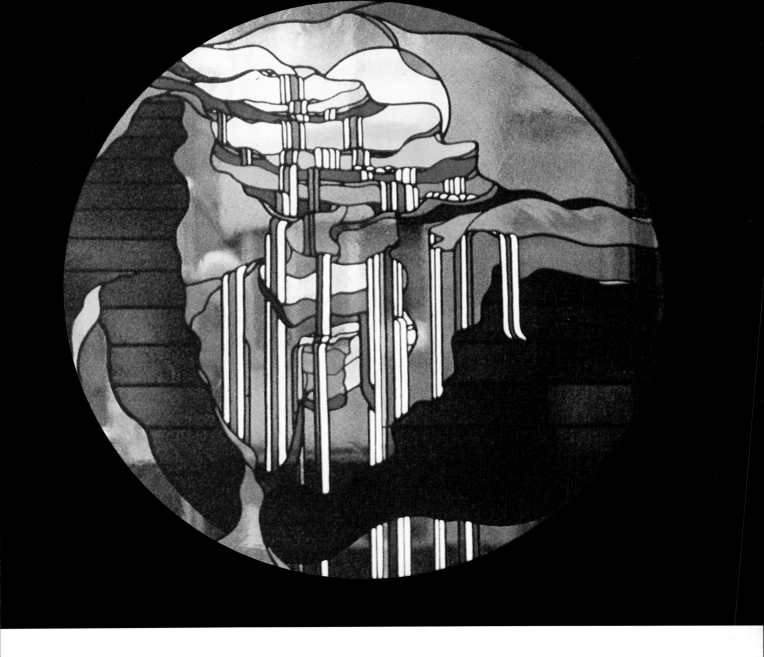

## Cascades

*Size:* 107 cm (3'6'') diameter
*Glass:* Antique
*Technique:* Leadlight

When working on a window with this type of design (many small pieces of glass and many of them parallel), you would be well advised to solder as you go or have a few small sheets of plate glass to put over the completed leaded work to hold it down. This is especially important when building your window tightly, and if you are using small or thin lead you will need to build tightly.

I give the warning because while building this particular panel, halfway through it exploded, and we literally had a hundred pieces of glass all over the floor, not to mention the days of work lost. At the time I had a very public studio and apart from the lost time it was very embarrassing as we ventured forth into explicit and appropriate superlatives, to find a gallery full of nice old ladies standing there, staring at our great mess with many quaint smiles as if nothing had really happened. I was extremely thankful to think that they must have been hard of hearing—although I presumed!

39

## Yarrando

*Size:* 122 × 122 cm (4' × 4')
*Glass:* Antique
*Technique:* Leadlight

This particular window is in a small chapel, which is rustic yet modern. Note the use of crystals which have been copper foiled, then soldered into holes. These holes were previously ground into the glass with the use of the small head on a glass grinder.

This chapel is part of a spiritual learning centre and has a very simple Christian philosophy, much of which is based on Matt Fox's creation spirituality, but also opens its arms to other religious points of view—hence the use of symbols that reveal creation. You will find in your own work the need to develop a sensitivity to your client and the use of the setting.

The sun, the earth and the stars are our playground, they sustain our physical needs, they are our home, they are Creation in the spectacular. The sun's tremendous energy warms the earth and has provided a symbol of outpouring throughout the ages. The cross has been deliberately placed behind Creation to symbolise what is behind the Christian world, the unseen world which governs so-called reality.

Whether your client is Buddhist, Christian, Hindu or Taoist, work with them in good faith and I'm sure more work will come your way. Word spreads.

# Working with stained glass

## Environments

Over the years I have been asked to design for many environments—and some have been unusual, to say the least. Here I have offered some examples as an incentive. You may, after reading this, find many other places where stained glass can be used.

The obvious and familiar places include sidelights in entrance ways, doorlights and fanlights, feature windows in sitting rooms and dining rooms. It doesn't cost much to cut a hole in a sitting room wall and fill it with an appropriate work in stained glass. Skylights are a lovely place to use stained glass—the effect of sunlight throwing out masses of colour over a polished floor is an exquisite use of the medium.

I have put stained glass into cupboards fitted inside with a small fluorescent light which creates a lovely soft effect, providing a subtle mood in a dining and kitchen area.

Bathrooms are also a great place for stained glass. Just give a little attention to the type of glass used. Some Antique or transparent glass is obviously going to enhance your neighbour's appreciation of the human form. I would recommend the use of heavily textured clear and coloured Catheral glass or opalescent glass. Here and there you can work in a little Antique glass, but only in small pieces, widely separated, if you wish to hold to your privacy.

Stained glass partitions are an aesthetic and practical way of dividing space and some examples are given later in the book. *Dalle de virre* or slab glass floors with backing lights, and artificial or backlit feature internal walls can be a delight.

Mirrors can also be enhanced by the use of stained glass. You can make candle holders and lamps—Tiffany as well as contemporary shades. Boxes for jewellery, mobiles and trinkets are quite common and can look very attractive.

If you have access to a kiln, another world that can be opened up is that of glass fusing and slumping. In Australia this particular endeavour is a rapid growth industry and I will touch on it toward the end of the book.

But most importantly, stained glass enhances the place where you live, work or play. The pure colours of stained glass pouring out into your favourite living space can change and uplift the surrounding atmosphere. Imagine a great host of angelic beings coming to life in your living room, in their hands the most precious jewels you have ever seen. All of a sudden, as if the brightest sun had just come from behind a cloud, the light of these jewels begins to dance with great subtlety across your life—that is the magic of light. Mix light with stained glass and you have created a great jewel, a great phenomenon that has blessed, uplifted and danced across the lives of humanity for some one thousand years. In your own home and work areas you also have an opportunity to bring these great jewels to life, for yourself and for generations to come, bringing light and colour into their lives.

## Handling glass and lead

There are many types of stained glass and quite a few different methods used in the making of them. Mouth blown, machine made and hand-rolled are the most common, providing the bulk of the stained glass utilised in stained glass studios.

Stained glass comes in many colours and textures, opaque and translucent. I strongly advise that you make yourself familiar with all the materials available before designing your own stained glass works.

Stained glass can be painted, it can be heated or fired, bent and melted. It can be heated to a plastic-like softness, slumped and manipulated to create unusual shapes. It can be cast like metal and it can be used with other materials to create new works of interest and inspiration.

There are a few rules to be aware of when handling stained glass.

The first is obvious: Stained glass comes in rectangular sheets roughly 1200 × 800 to 1000 mm in size and should be *handled with great care*. I have seen a sheet being held up to the light for observation break up in the person's hands and rain down in bits and pieces (some large) over his head. He was very luckily not too badly hurt. When working with glass, especially when cutting, always wear shoes—even a small piece of glass can bite deeply if accidentally dropped on one's toes. You may think this is too obvious even to mention but I have had many students come to classes wearing sandals and, on a few occasions, thongs.

Always keep a small *first aid kit* handy—Band-aids, tweezers, cotton buds, eye wash and a needle. This is not to say that accidents are frequent—in my experience they are not—but small nicks are common and must be expected. As I have said before, I have not witnessed a bad cut in all my time working and teaching in this field.

### Lead came

Today most lead is pre-stretched, comes in nicely packaged boxes and is a pleasure to work with. There are a myriad shapes and sizes, many available from most stained glass suppliers.

Lead ties all your glass together. A lot of thought needs to be given to the size you use—consider the strength and structure of your stained glass panel, especially where the work is going to face the direction of bad weather.

*Safety precautions when working with lead:* Everyone—students and professionals—should wash their hands with soap at the end of a session working with lead. Don't smoke and work with lead at the same time. Don't eat and work with lead. These are rules strictly to be adhered to.

*Toxicity:* If I have a student who is pregnant I always advise her to build her work in copper foil (a different technique to leadlight altogether). If she is insistent on working in lead I advise her to purchase surgical gloves from the chemist and to wear them when handling the lead. I also advise pregnant women working in copper foil to wear gloves when soldering and have a well ventilated room to rid the air of solder fumes,

as solder has a lead content as well. I know of only one professional who has suffered from lead poisoning. He disobeyed all the rules and ended up in hospital for three months. All other workers in the industry I have asked, including many who have regular blood tests and are handling lead almost every day, have little or no increase in blood lead levels compared with the person in the street—although these days it probably depends on what street!

# Reinforcing—a new way

If one looks back at the stained glass of past centuries, traditional reinforcing was quite visible and reasonably effective. Most stained glass was built in small panels and the panels placed together to form a whole window. Steel bars were fitted horizontally into the (stone) frame, placed to join glass sections together. The sections were then tied with small pieces of wire, soldered to the stained glass panels beforehand. In fact it is not uncommon to see reinforcing bars cut right across the human form and other main elements—on the odd occasion I have seen bars cutting through faces, which has always amazed me.

Recently stained glass has taken some small steps into the twentieth century with a new development in the reinforcing procedure. This new procedure uses steel bars that have been hot dipped in tin. This enables the steel to be soldered to the lead came; with the use of the small jig shown in the photograph, the steel can be bent to the shape of the lead line, which brings into being a reinforcing that allows the flow of line and colour to go unimpeded and gives us the opportunity to build our stained glass panels to a much larger size than before. Once these bars have been coated with some flat black paint they virtually disappear.

I think it is most important to solder these steel bars at 15–23 cm (6'–9'') intervals. But first you will need to tin (solder) the areas of the bar you wish to solder to the lead came. The steel bar is not easy to solder until you have put some heat into it. So firstly, place the bar over the lead came you would like to solder it to. Mark the spots on the bar you wish to solder. Take the bar away and hold the soldering iron on the marked spot, putting heat into the bar. Now, flux and solder. Just a thin layer of solder is all that's necessary for the time being. Place the bar in its position on top of the came, flux the corresponding points on the lead and solder to your heart's content. Where the iron bars meet, solder them to the came and solder the bars together as well. I have also bolted bars together as an added precaution, especially on large works such as the window shown on the cover and pages 12–13.

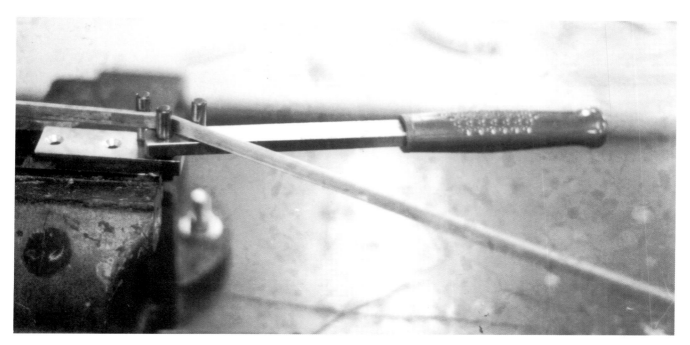

This jig is used to bend the steel bar which is fashioned for reinforcing the stained glass panels. It is very easy to use but the whole process of reinforcing in this way is enormously time consuming

# Enlarging a design

There are many ways of enlarging the drawings in the back of the book to suit your own project. The easiest is to measure the size of your window or space and take the drawing you want to use and the measurements of that space to a copy centre. Not all but most will have machines or facilities for architects. Among these will be a machine that can not only enlarge drawings up to huge sizes accurately, but can also distort the shape—in other words, vary the width or height to your requirements.

The other way, and always a good one to learn, is to graph the work up or draw a grid. This is simply done by dividing the drawing up into sections. First of all take the top and bottom horizontal lines and divide them into 8 equal parts. Now take the left and right vertical lines and divide them into 4 equal parts. Draw lines between the corresponding top and bottom points, and lines between the left and right points. There should now be a graph over your design. For the cartoon draw up the exact size space you wish to build into and perform the same procedure, in other words divide the horizontals into 8, the verticals into 4. Proceed to draw your design onto the cartoon freehand using the graphed design as your guide. You do not have to use the 4 to 8 ratio, you can use 6 to 12, 10 to 20, or 20 horizontal, 40 vertical. The larger increment may be necessary if your work is large and complex.

One other easy way of enlarging your design to cartoon size is to photocopy your drawing or pencil sketch onto film. Most photocopiers will do this. You will now need an overhead projector to project the drawing onto the cartoon paper. I have found this method to be somewhat wanting in the area of accuracy, so you may need to fudge your way through. What I have sometimes done is use the overhead projector to give me a rough idea of my drawing, usually sketching very lightly with pencil, then taking the cartoon to the bench and redrawing areas that have become distorted or elongated. It is not the most accurate way of drawing up your cartoon but if you are working on something that is extremely complex it will give you an idea of where you are going with your design very quickly.

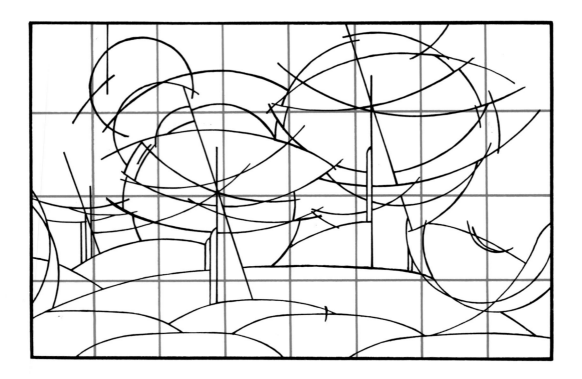

The complete design with grid drawn over it (above), and below, the enlarged grid with partly copied design

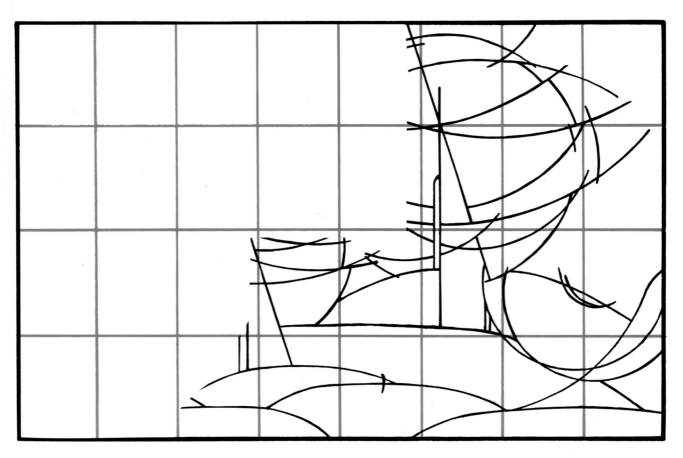

# Designs

The stained glass windows on pages 12–40 are a small portion of my own works to be used just as an educative tool in design, and as an inspiration as to what can be achieved with stained glass. They may also provide a starting point for thought, looking at of some of the problems that may come up during the process of designing and building.

The design guidelines on the following pages will help you with general principles of design; following them come numerous coloured and outline designs for your use.

# Design guidelines

## No. 1   Where to begin

When I first started designing stained glass, I had no previous training or knowledge and basically began by drawing upon the inspirations of other artists. I looked at a myriad stained glass books, studied many designs that I found interesting and began to use these works as a basis for my own sketches. Out of this came my own development, and henceforth my own individual style.

So my first advice to the beginner designer is to look out for a broad cross-section of work, study the styles and even practice using these works as a basis for your own drawing. I certainly have no objection to you utilising my own stained glass works as a foundation for study. That is partly the reason for this book.

## No. 2   Get a feeling for the space

Every environment is unique. I sometimes stand or sit for a long time in front of a window, paying particular attention to the architecture, the colours inside and out. I look at what is outside, whether it be a tree or a red brick building, maybe even a telegraph pole—they all play a role in determining what is appropriate for this particular space. Also take into account the people who will be or are utilising the building, as well as the reason for the building's existence. Then take all this back to the drawing board. I quite often take photographs of the buildings, the frames and the room to help me with my design work.

## No. 3   Drawing to scale

The first thing to remember when designing for stained glass is that you are designing (generally) for a specific space and size. Your completed window has to fit into a frame that is solid, therefore you must design and build to fit with great accuracy. So I always design to scale, 1:10, 1:20, whatever, depending on the size of the work. If you have scored the commission of your life, 50 metres × 16 metres (150' × 50'), you may have to work 1:30. But whatever the scale, make sure you measure the frame accurately and draw your initial sketch with the same degree of accuracy, to scale.

## No. 4   Initial sketches

People have many and varied approaches to design. I like to work initially just with a pencil and an eraser. When I first started I was terribly slow. With so much to be mindful of, I would start out just working on a line drawing, not even thinking much about colour. The process was arduous. I would then trace my original and begin colouring in. Now I have access to a photocopier and I take two or three copies of my original sketches. I think in colour when I'm drawing and find this saves a great deal of time. It makes it a lot easier if you can develop a concept in your mind before starting the process of drawing.

When, for example, you want to sketch something traditionally Federation and simple, the process of drawing is taken step by step. Generally you will have a border, the design will probably be symmetrical, and as long as you have achieved a nice balance with a few flowers (or whatever motif you choose), your design cannot go wrong. You can work up something that is asymmetrical; this is marginally a little harder in which to achieve balance but still reasonably easy for the beginner.

When you are drawn to contemporary design as I am, you are opening up a whole new set of problems. Abstraction to me is a very exciting world and I feel one has to start drawing with a freedom in the hand, a looseness that will allow free movement, free flow, and yet you must still *be aware* of all the technical restraints—that is, what is sound structure, what can and can't be cut, and so on. One exercise I often ask my students to perform, especially when I sense they are freezing up and becoming too tense, is to take a piece of blank paper and draw a frame. Then I tell them to shut their eyes and start scribbling over the framed area. When they have finished, I tell them to rub out all the lines which went outside the border, and pin the work up on a wall. You can do this too. Now, stand back and look. Study the shapes, the flow of rhythms, the flow of lines. Work out what is important to you, and begin to erase that which is of no value. Re-work the lines and shapes that seem promising and, with some thought for structure and consideration for colour, bring your drawing exercise to its completion. If you are really excited about the outcome, put colour to your work and see where you end up. This is only one way of loosening up, and yet I have witnessed some wonderful results from students. For those people who have been trained in art or design I probably need say no more, although the above exercise has also been of value to some students that were trained.

**Beginning the colouring process:** Watercolour, oils, crayons and inks are all good tools for use in design work. I generally use inks myself because they're bright and can be mixed or thinned down with water with some ease.

Those people who paint may like to work up a design first using oils or acrylics, but be very aware of structure as you work on your design. I have touched on problems of structure on pages 42 and 48; it would be advisable to read this section before getting stuck into your first painting or design.

In contemporary work there are no design rules, only *technical restraints*. For my own enjoyment I err on the side of refinement and balance, and yet I love seeing passionate work when the need or environment calls for it.

When you begin to sketch or paint be aware of some of the things we have touched on so far:

the structure of the building
what the facility is to be used for
the type of people who will use the space—old, young, conservative, etc.
what's inside—colours, furnishings, etc.
what's outside—poles, wires, trees, etc.
budget

Remember that you will have to install the window and the cost of that must be included in the overall budget. You do need to think about installation, even at the initial drawing stage; apart from budget considerations you will need to keep in mind structure and how it (the stained glass) will be fitted.

**Leadlines:** In traditional stained glass design the emphasis was on intense colour and the context or content of the window. In contemporary work colours are not necessarily the main concern—colour is married to the importance of line work and in some cases to the texture and movement in the glass itself. So when thinking line, think thick or very thin. Lead can be bought across the counter in thicknesses from 3 mm to 25 mm, and 25 mm is a mighty thick line to play around with. Experiment putting thick and thin lines together (see page 13); use what's there to its fullest advantage.

**Colour:** For me colour is a difficult subject to write about, especially when it comes to guidance and opinions. The world of colour is so subjective that I don't want to make too many statements about what can be considered right or wrong. But I would suggest that you be mindful of where your window will finally live. If it's a hospital, think of colours and forms that are restful, peaceful, healing. I have a slide which I sometimes show my students to make this precise point. I generally ask first up what this window represents, how it makes them feel, and to date I have always had more or less the same feedback, that is, it's violent, it's passionate, it's awful, it's exciting but disturbing. It is a slide of a window at the end of a hospital ward in the United States. When I tell my students this they certainly get the point. I personally like the window but as an exhibition piece—its position at the moment in a place of healing I think is totally wrong. So be mindful of the facility, especially when it comes to colour and form. There are many books available on colour and how it works together. If you wish to pursue more knowledge in that area look at *The Elements of Colour* by Itten.

**Texture:** Texture is increasingly playing an important role in stained glass work. Because of this new direction, glassmakers have responded by bringing out new ranges of heavily textured glasses. Spectrum Reamy is one such product to be considered but look for others as well—Bullseye, Wissmach, Desag, to name a few. If you are working on a design that captures the movement of the ocean or even ripples in a pond, look around for a glass with swirling textures. Use the texture as part of your design. You may wish to hint at carrying on the swirling movement into the next but different piece of glass by the use of a little trace paint or false leading.

**Fusing and slumping:** Fusing glass together in a kiln is another possible way of enhancing your stained glass. If you have access to a kiln you are on the road to opening up another design attribute and maybe a new endeavour in the glass arts. Think about the potential of leading into your design a section of fused glass, maybe even as the focal point of the design. Slumping glass over moulds to create three-dimensional forms is also worth pursuing. These forms can then be worked into your stained glass panel. Fusing and slumping glass is not a difficult procedure if you know a few of the rules, and there are numerous books on the subject available at stained glass suppliers. I have also touched on the subject at the back of this book for your interest (page 101).

### No. 5  What to do when you're stuck

I almost tossed a coin as to whether I would include this section, so I do hope it is of some value.

For me the whole process of dealing with a design crisis has taken some time to develop. Many people will find their own way of handling the build-up of intensity when a design has come to a grand dead end, and I can assure you that will be an inevitable event as you develop along the road to greater skill in your drawing. I have now come to the point of knowing that whatever problem arises, given time and careful consideration it can be sorted out.

Firstly, when you get stuck, leave the room, take a walk, make some tea, or work on something completely different. When you arrive back at your drawing you will see things in the design you have not noticed—you will discover lines that don't work, areas that all of a sudden excite you, and so on. If all else fails, sit somewhere favourable, quietening your mind and feelings; sit there for ten or fifteen minutes, paying attention to your thoughts and the surrounding noises. Be aware of your entire body and you will eventually experience or sense a quietness, at which time feel your way back into the design problem and with any luck you will come to some answers. I'm sure you'll have some success with this technique.

Sometimes I have to remind myself that in the whole scheme of things this particular work of mine is somewhat insignificant. That usually brings a good laugh and puts the whole thing in its proper perspective. At times having fun while working and not taking all this too seriously is as important as eating.

## No. 6    Budget

Every job is different when it comes to sorting out all the costs to be incurred. Generally I work from a simple guide—20% design fee, 20% materials, 50% wages, including installation, and a 10% margin for those little things that do go wrong from time to time and/or profit. When it comes to large scale work you will need to reassess this simple breakup of budget requirements. You may find that a 10% slice (which could amount to $10 000) is all the budget can afford for design fee. You may need to create large areas of little colour, including very large pieces of unbroken glass, to meet your budget requirements for a very large work. Whatever the size of the commission, do give this area some considerable thought.

When considering your initial concept it is always important to keep in mind your access to glass and its cost. It's so easy to blow a budget when seduced by the wonderful colours and textures of those many sheets of glass that the importer just happens to have lying around in the light for your enjoyment as you enter the shop. I'll go into this area a little later on in the book.

## No. 7    Glass supplies

It's prudent to be aware that glass shops often will not have the colour or texture you require to complete your masterpiece. When choosing your glass be aware of how many sheets the wholesaler has in stock, because it's extremely frustrating being two-thirds of the way through a job, running out of glass, and finding that the shop is out of stock of the essential colour or glass type that you have been using. On one particular project this happened to us in a memorable way—because of an agreed installation time we had to replace all the glass we had already cut to maintain uniformity throughout the work. So, be careful!

## No. 8    Design and structure

This is an area of great significance. The main theme of this book is design and how to begin—plus you have the use of my designs in the last section. So, I don't wish to go into too much technical detail on how to build stained glass, but I do wish to add a word of caution, especially when it comes to structure. Use your commonsense and be mindful of structure as you design. A conference I attended some years ago at Sydney University opened my own eyes to some of the problems we faced in the industry when poor design skill, married to bad cementing technique (that is, waterproofing and stabilising the window), led to some stained glass works in Sydney buckling, cracking and leaking within six months of installation. Now I don't want to over-concern you—I am simply asking that you give some thought to this problem as you go along. To help while you work, remember that every third to half square metre (3 to 6 square feet) will need reinforcing. Some sidelights may not require reinforcement because you have glass running from one side of the frame to the other which in itself is reinforcement enough.

One of the questions you will need to ask as you move through the design process is 'Will the window warp over a period of time?' Look at the dynamics of your design. With some careful thought you will begin to see how the window will bend over the years under the influence of wind, rain, storms, gravity and building movement—yes, building movement. All buildings move and this is definitely an area to be mindful of as you are growing in your design skill. Another point to look at is that any stained glass that sits beside an entrance way, for example, a sidelight, is going to suffer the bangs and slams of a myriad human beings in all sorts of moods. Some of those bangs may be of great force. I was called to one job years ago to quote on a repair. When I asked what had happened, I was told that the man of the house just happened to put his fist, with some force I might add, right through the stained glass. Giving some thought to the job I was glad that the so-called 'man of the house' was not home.

Well, on this occasion there was not much one could have done to prevent this new shape in the stained glass, but generally, given some careful thought, most stained glass window warp can be avoided in the design stage by the use of appropriate reinforcing. If you are in doubt take your design to someone in the industry and have them check your work. I'm sure most professionals would be glad to help.

In this section I have included a number of designs for your use. You may copy them, enlarge them or distort them for your own needs and to suit your own space. Some I have shown in colour, some just as line drawings. The coloured drawings are only offered as an idea—you may colour them as you see fit.

I have placed the simpler designs at the beginning of this section; as we move on toward the end of the book they become increasingly complex.

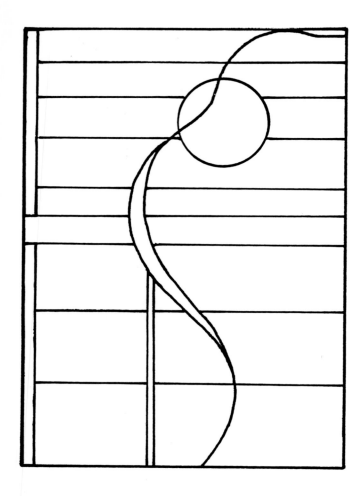

Exceedingly simple design, slight Japanese flavour to it, very easy to build. A good one to get you started.

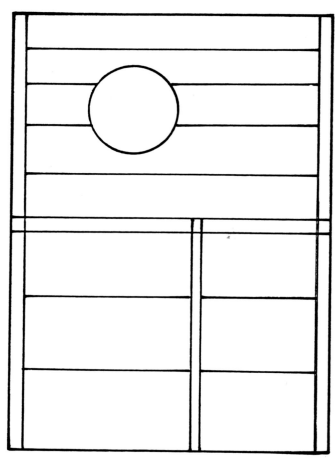

Simple and easy to build sidelight (or for whatever small space you have). You can utilise just the top section if that is closer to the size of your window opening.

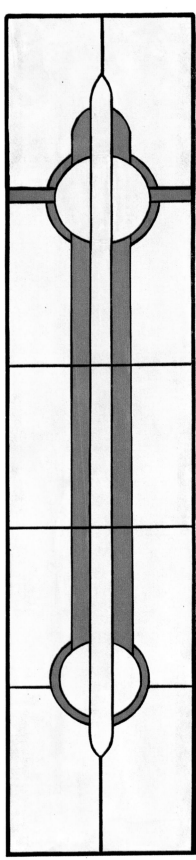

Also a quite simple design, an easy to build sidelight. Remember though that you can take a simple design and create something very lovely by choosing your glass well. Simplicity and a good Antique glass can do wonders.

This entrance way is plain yet agreeable to the eye, easy to build and I am sure will please you when installed. Change the colouring as you wish.

Opposite:
This double sidelight has a few curves but is still an easy one to build. Just be sure to put a couple of reinforcing bars across the horizontals about one-third and two-thirds of the way up the window.

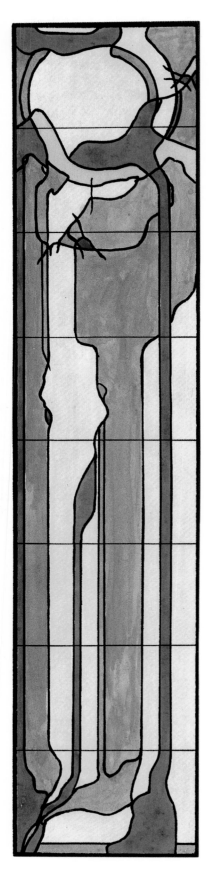

You can turn this design into sidelights, a partition, a feature window in your lounge room wall, etc. Change the colours to suit, change or play around with the design if you think you can enhance it. I would also add a couple of reinforcing bars to be on the safe side. Another version appears on page 74.

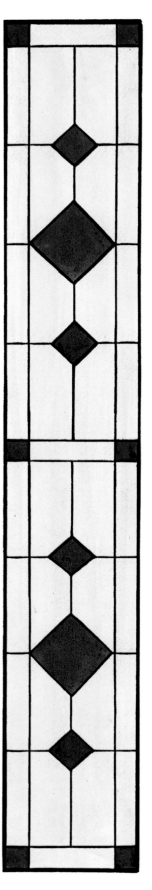

Elementary sidelight. You can use just the top panel if need be. I would place a bar across one of the centre horizontals if building the whole window.

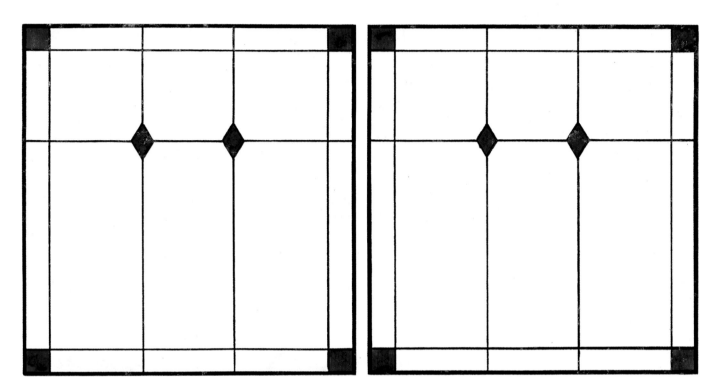

Kitchen windows—simple, but with the use of Antique glass they would
be quite elegant, especially if you are facing out into a beautiful garden.

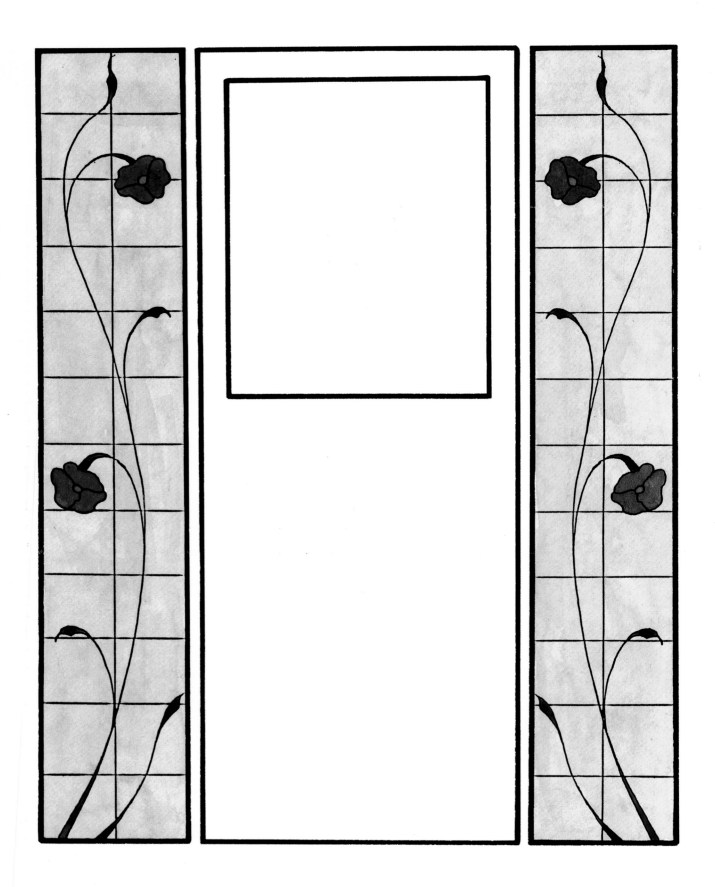

Opposite:
A few curves in this but with some care you should be able
to manage it with just a couple of practice pieces under your
belt. Don't forget a reinforcing bar or two.

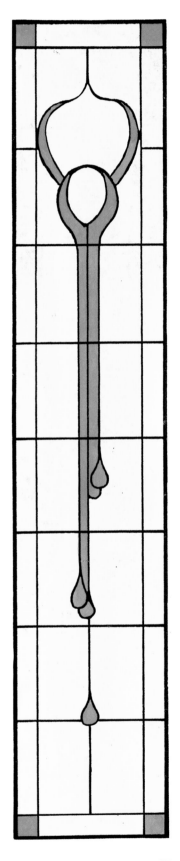

This design is a play on the theme on page 51.

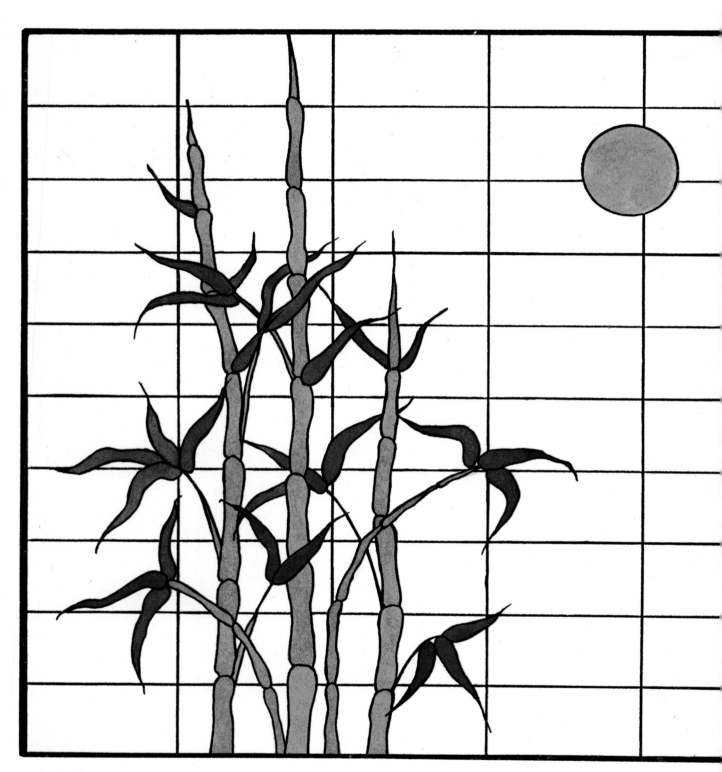

With this design the placement possibilities are numerous. I designed it with a partition in mind but it could be used in many other situations. When building this work be very careful to make sure the horizontal and vertical lines are nice and straight. With this basic bamboo drawing and/or partition you can cut it down, or enlarge it.

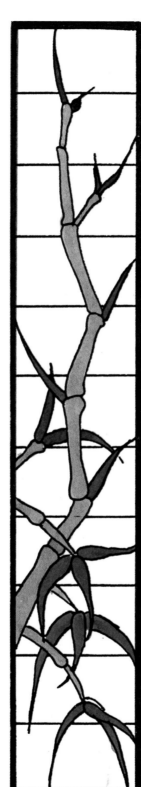
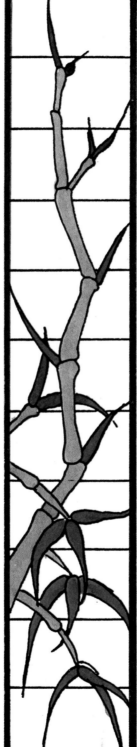
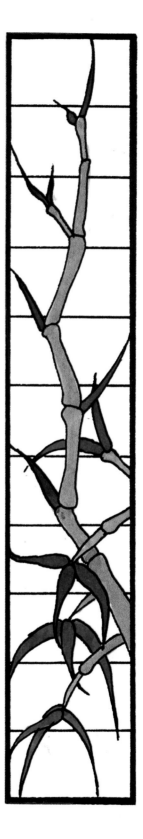

Double or single sidelights designed to go
with the bamboo partition.

A bathroom would be a fitting place for this design. See how the colour and line moves from one side to the other. If you wish to bring these windows closer together (if the space between the panels is a smaller proportion than I have allowed) you will have to pay some attention to the lines and colour that move from one panel to the other. Only a minor adjustment will need to be made. Trace the drawing with a pencil, re-arrange the appropriate lines so that they work or run from one side to the other, rub out the old lines and there you have it. These windows are not big, so if you wish to place them into a large space you will need to give some thought to breaking a few of the pieces up as well as adding some reinforcing.

Sidelight, reasonably easy to build, just change the colours to suit. Variations of this design appear on pages 80 and 81.

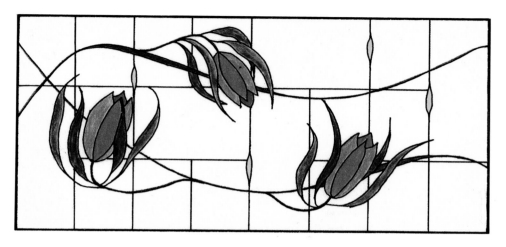

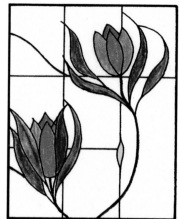

Entrance way. Try to keep the leadline as thin as practicable except in the stem itself. I think the flowers should look as delicate as possible.

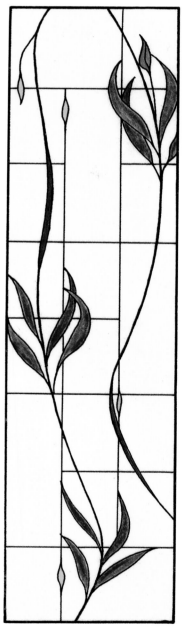

A contemporary design based on the Blue Mountains' Hanging Rock. This is pretty straightforward—just be thoughtful when choosing glass. I would tend to look for some nice textures as well as streaky glass, for example.

All the designs in this next section are straightforward. Work with them as you see fit. They can be photocopied, coloured in and/or changed to your heart's content. Just be sure to think about structure as you play around with these drawings.

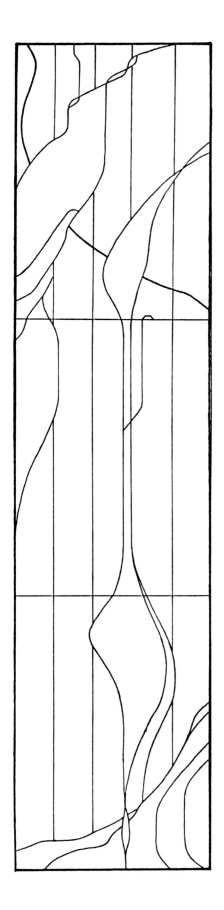

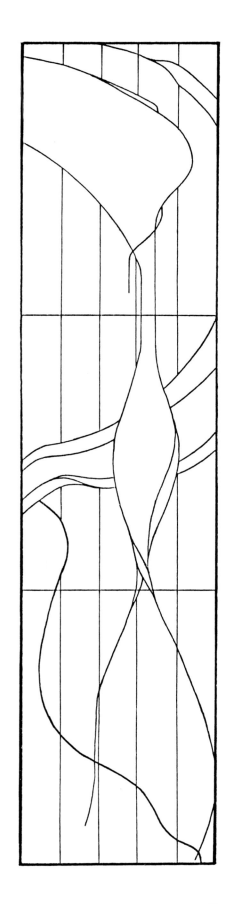

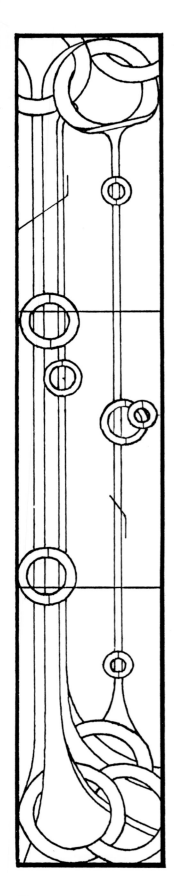
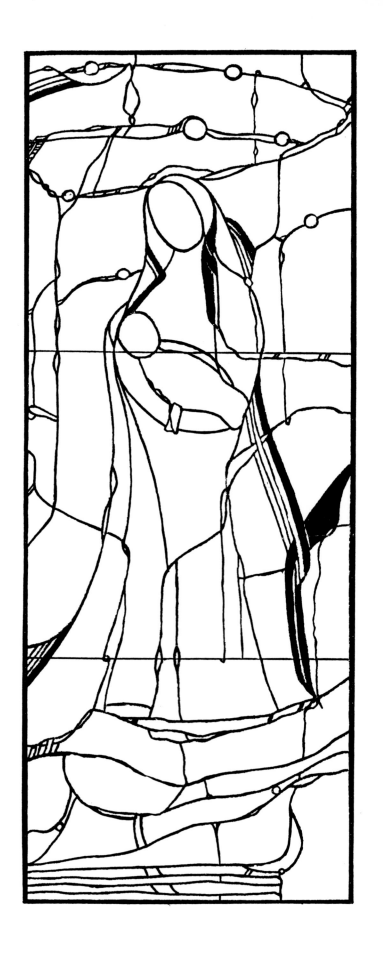

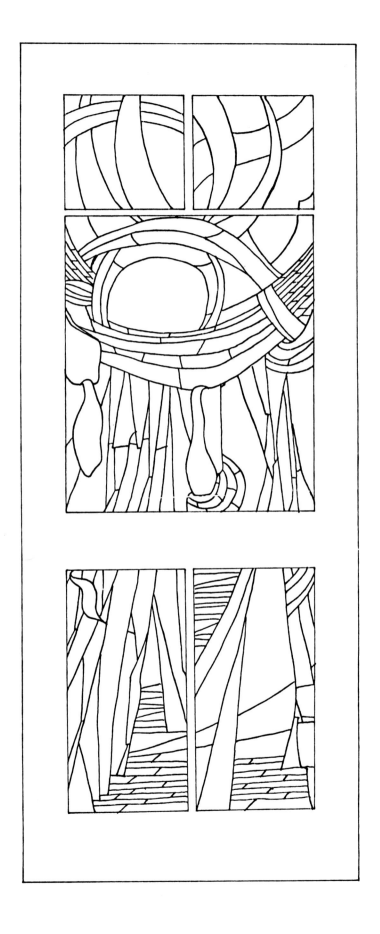

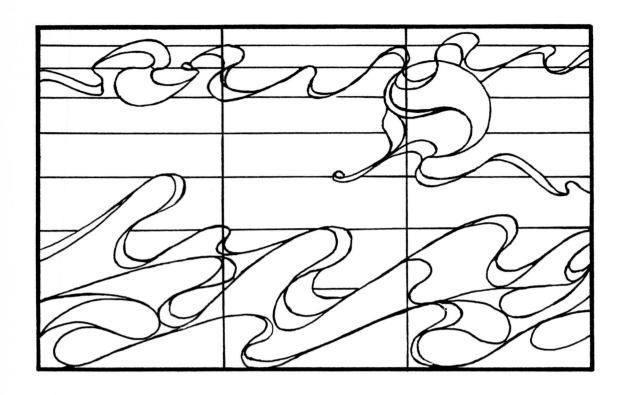

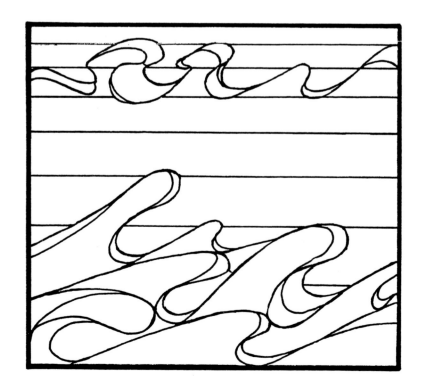

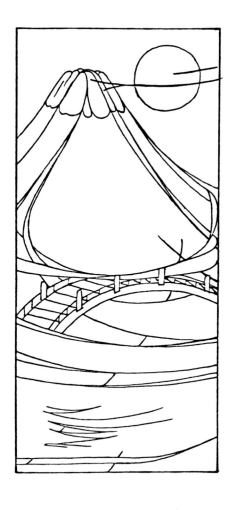

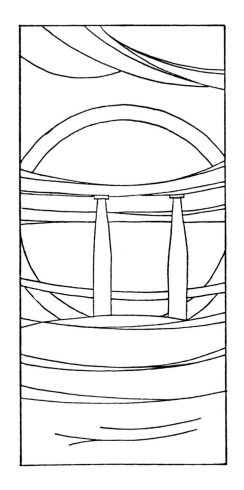

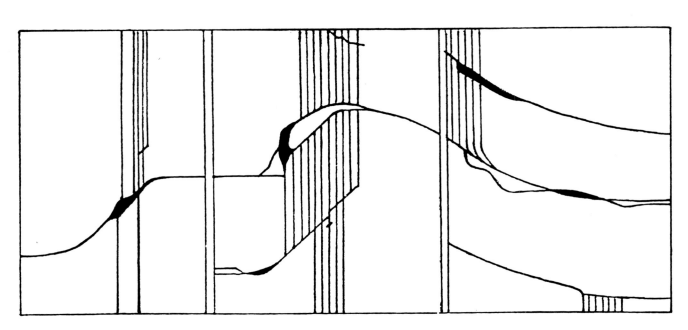

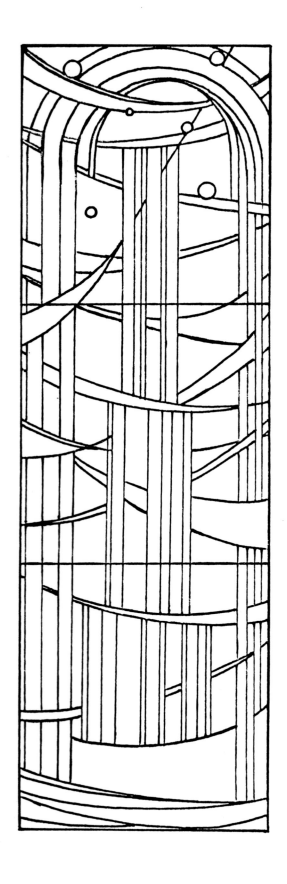

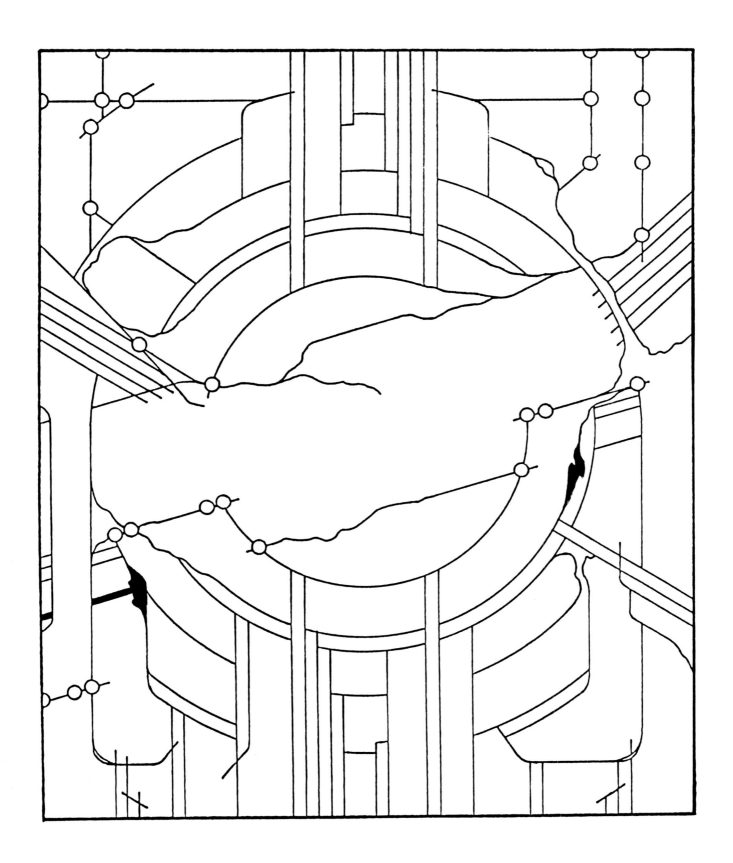

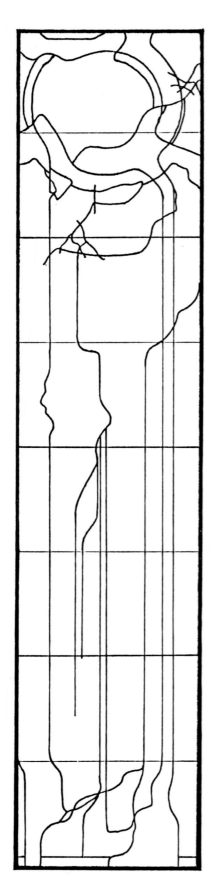

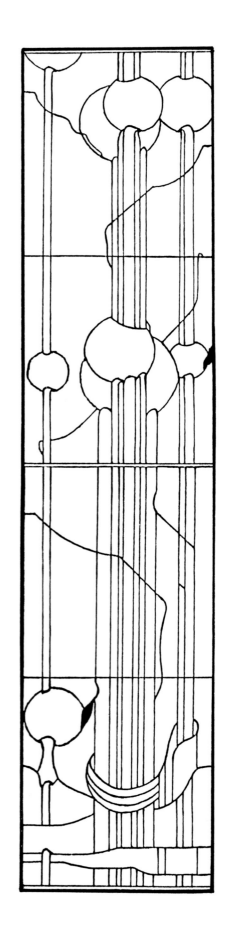

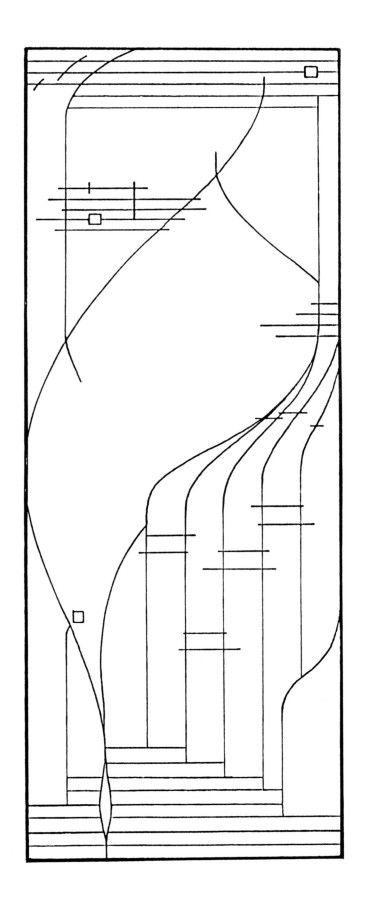

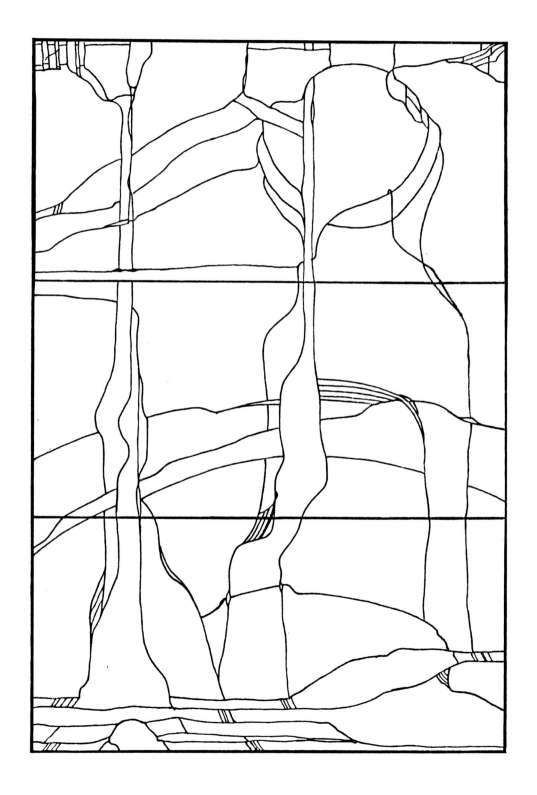

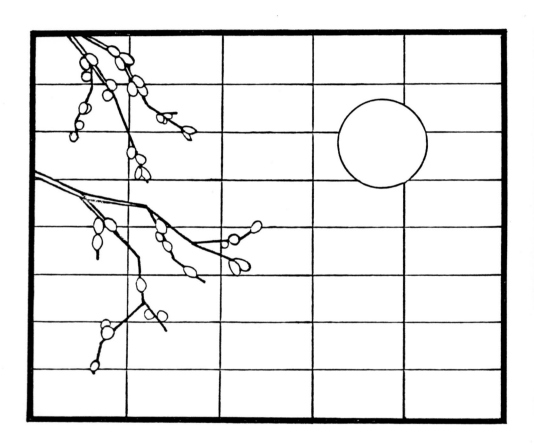

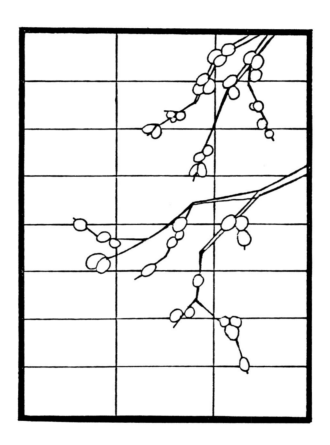

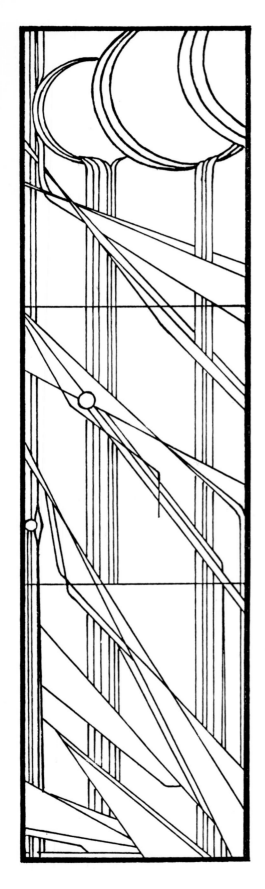

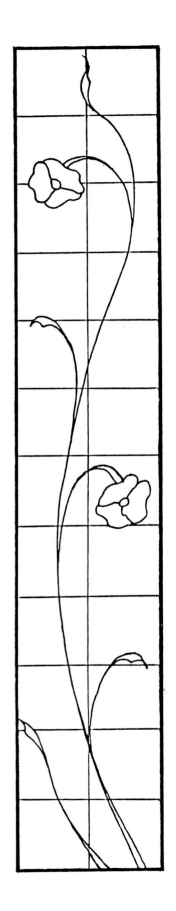

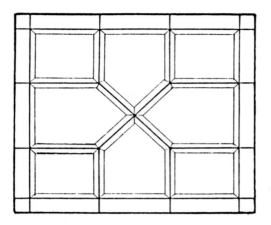

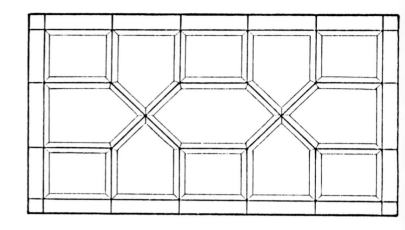

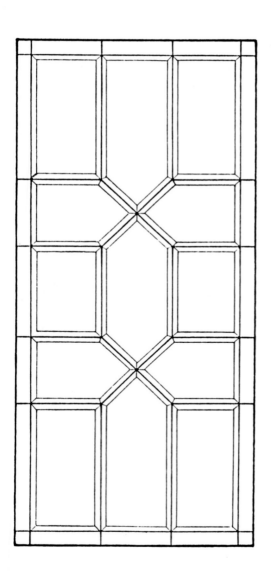

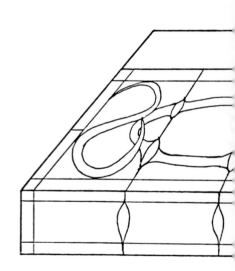

This snooker table lamp can be enlarged or reduced according to the dimensions of your table. You will need to pay particular attention to the shadow this or any shade will throw. It will simply be a matter of widening the lamp or raising it higher, so whatever you do construct a cardboard model before building. The frame can be made out of timber, steel, aluminium or even a strong moulded plastic, and don't forget, use opalescent or heavily textured glass because the last thing you want to see are the globes or fluorescent tubes.

Opposite:

I have offered this concept as a possibility for those people who have a desire to create a bevelled glass entrance or sidelight. The procedure is quite simple. If you understand the basic principles of stained glass technique you will find great pleasure in making a bevelled window. All you need is 6 mm clear float glass. Cut it to the design's requirements. Then take the glass to a bevelling expert to be run through a specialised bevelling machine. If you keep your design to straight lines, you will save yourself a lot of expense with the bevelling as any rounded sections have to be worked by hand. Once the glass is bevelled, the process of building is the same as for stained glass. Just be aware that the glass is 6 mm thick on the unbevelled sections, so you will need to use a lead came with a fairly wide channel in these areas.

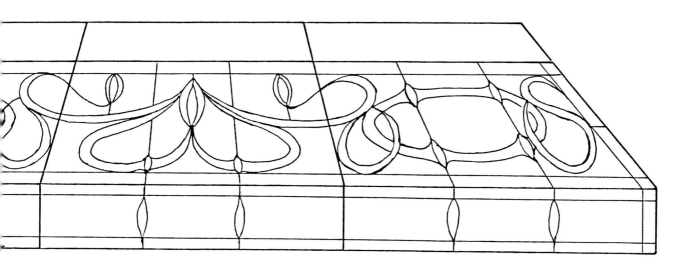

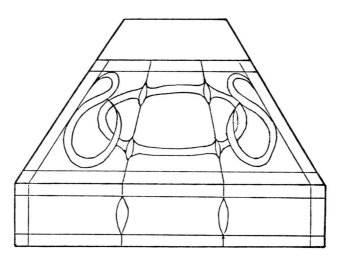

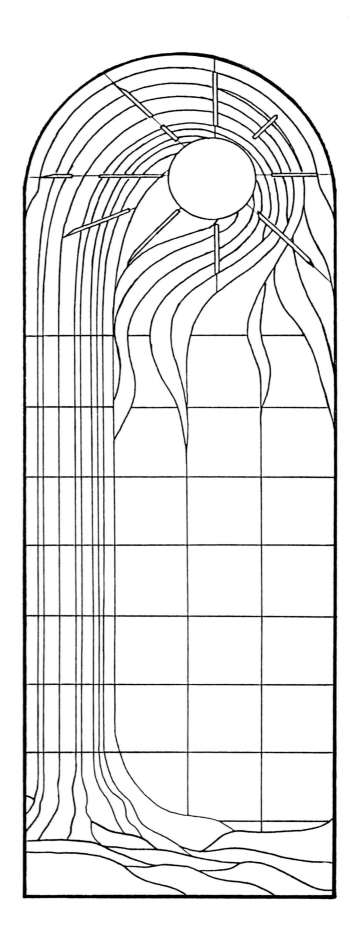

I placed these designs here as examples of working with specific symbolic needs and specific places. It's important to take on the thoughts and feelings of your client and work with them to the best of your ability. Some of these designs have been built, but not always in the exact form shown here.

## Untitled

*Size:* 762 × 122 cm (25' × 4'), 2 panels

These two designs were created for a modern church to represent two different styles, one complex, the other quite simple, but were disregarded in favour of a more traditional work. I have included them because the style may be of some interest. The colours here are pencil colours sprayed with a gloss protective coating to bring out a more intense pigment, in an attempt to get closer to the colour intensity of stained glass.

These are the initial colour sketches.

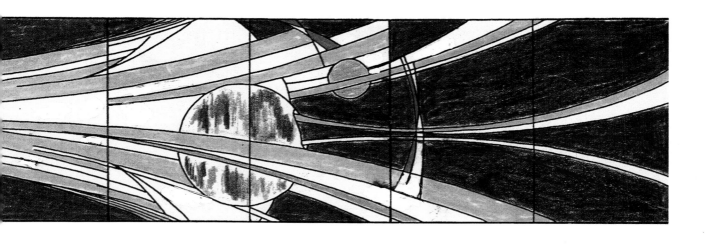

## Untitled

*Size:* 762 × 152 cm (25' × 5')
*Glass:* German Antique and French Antique
*Technique:* Leadlight

This design was created for a private school in Sydney. It incorporates the four house badges and the main school badge or emblem. The brief was simply to include or design these particular items into an overall concept that was both modern and within the required budget. The first, I'm happy to say, we achieved, but unfortunately we did manage to go slightly over budget, which on a project of this size can easily happen, especially when you happen to break one of the panels during installation! The design has a lot of false leading; we also used the new method of reinforcing, as well as painting, etching and laminating. My main reason for including this work was to show how one can take a number of symbols and marry them into a design concept that flows right across the entire width. With this design I began by setting out the frame, then placed the badges so they were balanced but not symmetrical. I then worked the design around them, starting at one end of the frame and working toward the other.

## Living Together

*Size:* 335 × 305 cm (11' × 10')
*Glass:* All Antique
*Technique:* Copper foil

I must say I really enjoyed working on this. Every now and then you will meet someone who will give you a free rein, as the headmaster of this particular school did. I found myself feeling quite passionate during the drawing process and sensed this was partly due to the confidence shown by the headmaster.

The window was placed in the entrance way of a library for young children. The symbols of the sun and solar system, the sky and the ocean are all tied together with living organisms, depicting Life as indivisible. Again you can see the use of false leadlines or copper foil lines adding to the free flowing style. We also laminated a few of the pieces because we could not find the glass colours we needed to complete the job. This process of laminating is quite easy and you can achieve some lovely effects when utilising different colours and textures. We also used our new reinforcing technique which added to the integrity of the flowing design.

## Untitled

Design only. Another example of what can be achieved with simplicity and a flowing line. This drawing was created for a religious building.

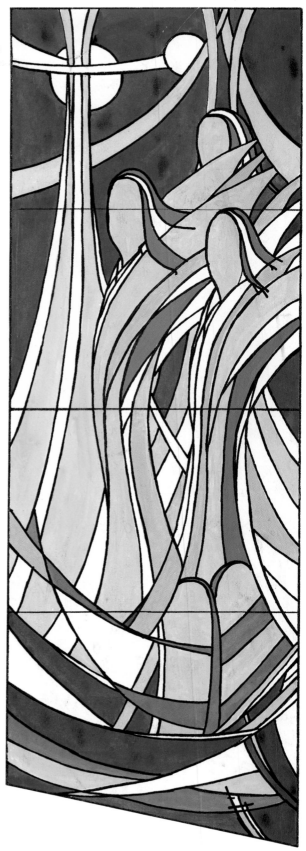

Opposite:
## The Sower and the Vine

*Size:* 213 × 61 cm (7' × 2'), 2 panels
*Glass to be utilised:* German Antique and French Antique; over 1000 pieces of glass
*Technique to be employed:* Leadlight with painted areas on the vine and the figure

This is an initial concept for a church in Sydney. The architect wanted something that would work with the existing windows but with a modern twist as the window is to be set into a new annexe of an old building.

This initial design will be worked up more fully as the cartoon is drawn, and areas to be matted will be shaded in. The concept is obvious inasfar as the sower and the vine were the two parables chosen by the church. The vortex which leads you to the central area in the window is symbolic of living in the world, sowing seeds, doing good things, but with a view or sense of heaven always there in the corner of one's eye.

## Untitled

Designed for spaces about 215 cm (7') in height.
Narrow windows, so I have emphasised the vertical lines,
pushing the colour up and outward. The two panels have
also been tied together by passing imaginary line and colour
across or through the space between. This is always an
important consideration when looking at multiple panels. You
would be surprised how easy it is to tie different panels together
by creating imaginary lines of colour across the space between
them and also by how effective and striking the result can be.

The designs in this section are more complex than the previous designs, and more open to your interpretation.

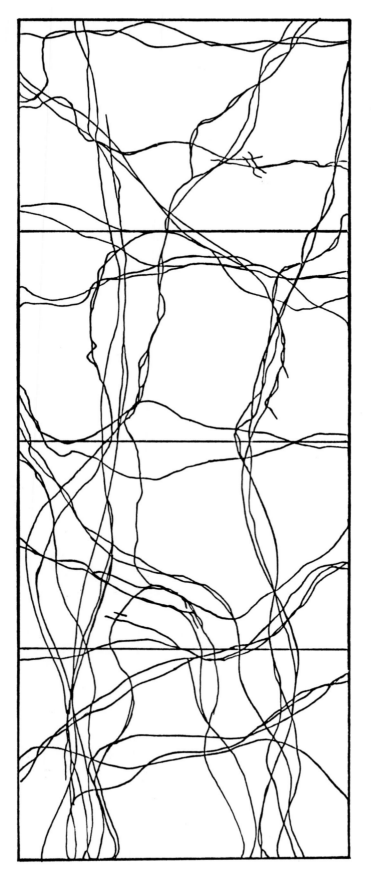

I have had a great time working up this design for you as I wanted to show you what can be done by taking a risk and really letting go with a pencil in your hand. As I have mentioned before, shutting your eyes and letting loose with your pencil when you are feeling a little uptight can lead to the most remarkable outcomes. In this particular exercise I did not close my eyes but really let loose with the pencil. It does have some potential and with a little work in the realm of colour, I'm sure you will come to an exciting project. If you look closely at the design you will see two emerging figures—one in the foreground, the other and much larger form in the background. Work your colour around to bring out these forms. If I was to build this window myself I would probably use copper foil and pay quite some attention to the size of line, increasing it to 25 mm where possible, just to emphasise certain areas.

I have found that when looking at Nature one can see all sorts of shapes—faces, for example—in rock formations, bark, lichen and so on. Treat your own scribblings with the same intense study and you will be surprised at what you see or have created.

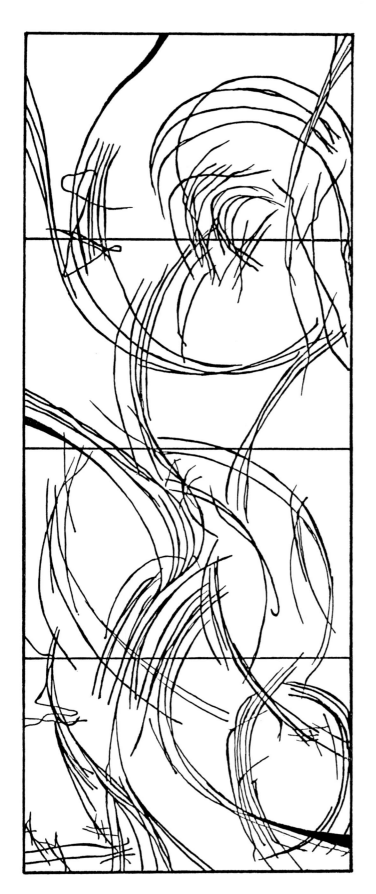

This is another of my not-so-serious attempts to design with some freedom in the hand. You will undoubtedly see a figure in the work which can be enhanced with the right accentuation of line and colour. I would be inclined to build this window using copper foil and accentuate the lines by enlarging and/or reducing them. I find this practice of using the line as a creative force very rewarding. One last thing to consider is the use of colour over the entire window. This is also a consideration for the other free flow design on page 96. What I would tend to mull over is the use of very little colour, allowing the line to dominate. The line is quite strong and can stand out on its own. Give some thought to little use of strong colour and work mainly with light tints. Just highlight the figure with some intensity, yet still keeping this within the bounds of subtlety. Epoxy is a great substance to use for fixing all the line overhangs to the glass. Solder the ends to the main copper foil work so they look to be part of the entire line composition. To make these extra lines one simply uses the face of the lead came, cut to the shape you desire. You can also solder over a strip of copper foil: first cut the length you require, fix it to a sheet of clear glass, flux, solder over the top and glue it into position. It is an easy procedure and will enlarge your design horizons.

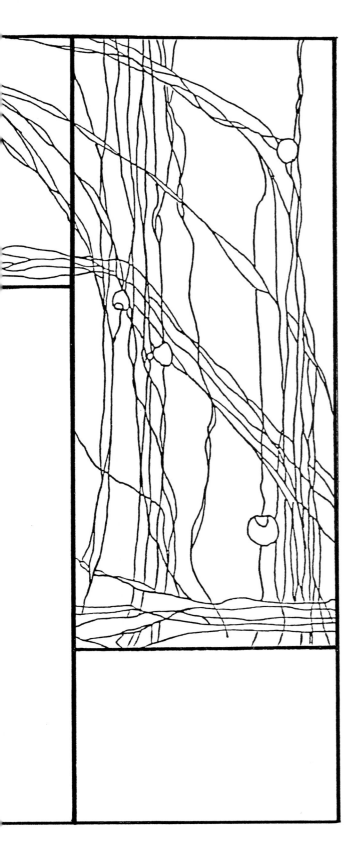

This drawing is an example of abstract symmetry, easily accomplished by photocopying a drawing onto clear film. In this case the left hand side was photocopied. I then took the film, turned it over and photocopied the original drawing alongside the film—hey presto! the finished design. You may wish to use only one side of the design or maybe just the left panel. With some attention to colour, I'm sure the design will work for you. Again in this window I would use copper foil to bind the glass and I would also keep the colour down, letting the line do most of the work.

I have offered this particular design, which was created for a space about 8 to 10 metres high, to open up one possible way of approaching a large work, religious in nature and contemporary in style. Here you can go for broke when it comes to colour. I'm not saying that every large religious work needs to be extremely colourful and busy; in fact, if you look at some of my large religious windows in this book you will note a sense of spaciousness, yet one does not have to go down this path every time. If I were building this window I would definitely use lead and keep those lines nice and straight. What I had in mind when drawing this was to work with dark colours at the base and move up the spectrum as I moved up the window, highlighting those long streaks from top to bottom with strong golds and yellows. The cross needs some attention in colour but I wouldn't highlight it too much. All the above are only suggestions so please don't feel bound by what I have said.

All the designs in the back of this book are for your own use. They are simply ideas for you to mull over, to look at how we can design a myriad different styles to suit the environment in which we are to place our work. If you think something needs to be changed then change it. Re-work the designs to your own satisfaction. At times I have spent up to one hundred hours on one drawing, agonising over one line or another, and have re-worked my colouring many times before being happy with the finished work. I think it is important not just for your client but also for yourself that you give your best to the task of designing and do not stop until you are really happy with the design. As I have said to my students many times, the hours are in the building as well as the expense, and I can assure you that it is very depressing to put many hours and hard work into something you feel is not quite right.

# Finale

I briefly mentioned the use of slumped and fused glass on page 47, and would now like to show you a sculptural work completed in 1989 in which I utilised the technique of slumping. This process is becoming extremely popular and many people are now turning to this work from flat glass because you can make small affordable pieces by the dozens and sell them at markets and the like. All you need is access to a small kiln, a little glass and some elementary training to get you on your way. Apart from making small bowls and plates, you can create your own glass or fuse together different colours to be leaded into stained glass.

## Purity of Spirit

*Size:* 396 × 305 cm (13' × 10')
*Weight:* 3.5 tonnes
*Material:* Glass prisms, granite, aluminium and steel
*Hours:* 2800

This sculpture is in a slightly different league to the run-of-the-mill use of slumped glass, but the technique utilised is basically the same—except that the kiln we used was over 15 metres (50') long. Being the first in Australia to bend glass this size we did strike a few problems in the beginning, but after three months experimentation we got it right and went on to slump 17 pillars or prisms, some weighing up to 82 kg (180 lb). The glass came from Italy—drawn glass slabs about 300 cm high, 183 cm wide and 32 mm thick (10' high, 6' wide and 1¼'' thick), very low in iron as they had been made originally for telescope lenses. We cut the slabs in five with a huge diamond saw, into pillars just over 30 cm (1') in width. After this we were off to another firm to bevel the edges all round to a five-sided facet. There was only one machine in the country that could do this and we happened to be only a few kilometres away from it.

After bevelling and polishing we were off to yet another firm with the only kiln in the state big enough to take the size and weight of our glass pillars, and it was here the real fun began. First of all we had a bit of a think-tank and pulled together the technical officers, engineers, works managers, mould makers, and began to plan our way through the next four months, not only scheduling but laying out all the problems we would have to confront and solve if we were to achieve our goal. And I might add that there were some problems we had not yet foreseen. The moulds were then made, and they were huge steel constructions which had to be lifted with a small crane.

Our first test went well excepting that the sheer weight of the glass, when soft enough to bend, forced itself into the perforations on the mould face and we lost it. Over two months we spent a few more sessions experimenting until we got it right. We had to get it right as some of the larger pillars cost up to $1000 each after bevelling had been completed. In fact, the bevel was one of the initial problems we had to overcome, that is, maintaining the nice sharp bevelled edge while heating the pillars to a point where they would bend. The bevel is responsible for breaking the light up into the natural spectrum visible in the photograph and therefore it is essential it be kept sharp.

After sorting out most of the foreseeable problems we bit the bullet and dived in. All went well for the most part. We were even lucky enough to have some professional stress testing, which was performed by a friend, a physicist with the CSIRO. Nonetheless, when we were three firings from the end of our project and only eight weeks from our unveiling time, drama!—and I mean real drama—one of the pillars exploded on leaving the main chamber. I was only thankful that no-one was injured. So, on the phone to call out the troops, and I must say that I was enormously impressed with the response from all those firms that were involved with the overall glass side of the process. Another pillar was ready for firing within four days. Then drama struck yet again—another pillar exploded.

We had one last pillar to complete, and this time I was really worried as I thought we were on the last of this glass left in the country. Luckily we did have enough to see us through and everyone got stuck in to finish the job. Six weeks later, all seven-day working weeks, we were finished.

I don't wish to discourage you at all but when attempting something new as we did here, you will need to sort out or overcome some unusual problems. I have found that with a cooperative effort and the desire to do something well from all concerned, these problems can surely be solved. So, here it is, installed and finished, and another possibility, maybe even a new horizon with glass. I hope you like the outcome.

One of the pillars (glass prisms) bending in the kiln

# Index

Abstraction, 46
Abstract symmetry, 99
Antique glass, 33

Bevelled glass, 8, 83, 102, 103
    design, 82
Bronze sculpture, 10
Budget, 30, 48
Building tightly, 39

Clear film, 99
Coefficient expansion, 20
Colouring/beginning the process, 46
Colour, 47
Communication, 16
Contemporary design, 46
Copper foil design, 14, 32, 33, 90
    use, 12
Cross, the, 29
Crystals, 40

*Dalle de virre*, 6, 21
Design and sculpture, 48
Designing, when you're stuck, 47
Design the new with the old, 93
    where to begin, 46
Drawing to scale, 46
Drawn glass, 102

Einstein, 10
Enhancing where you live, 41

Enlarging a design, 43
Environments, 41
Epoxied lead to glass, 13, 19
Epoxy, 97

Facet, 5 sided, 102
False lead, 97
False leading, 13, 19
False solder strips, 32, 33
Feeling for the space, 46
Federation, 46
First aid kit, 42
Footwear, 42
Fusing and slumping, 47

Glass globules, 12
Glass, handle with care, 42
Glass supplies, 48
Graph, 43, 44
Grid system, 43, 44

Hammer and chisel work, 6, 21
Handling glass and lead, 41

Imaginary line and colour across
    space, 94
Initial sketching, 46

Jig, 42, 43

Lead lines, 47

Leadlights, 13, 15–20, 22–31, 34–40
Lead toxicity, 42
Looking at nature, 96

Natural spectrum, 102

Painting, elementary examples, 24–6
Partition possibilities, 58
Photocopying on film, 43, 99
Prismatic effects, 8

Quieten your mind, 47

Reinforcing—a new way, 13, 24–6,
    28, 29, 43, 48
    new design, 90

Safety and lead, 42
Scribblings, 96
Silver stain, 24, 25
Slab glass, 6, 21
Slumping glass, 47, 102
Snooker lamp shade, 34
Snooker table lamp, 82
Structure, 21, 48
Symbolism tied into modern design,
    29, 37, 40, 88, 90

Texture, 47
Toxicity, lead and fumes, 42
Trace and mat work, 24–6